ABOVE THE MOON EARTH RISES

ABOVE THE MOON EARTH RISES

Hymn texts, anthems, and poems for a new creation

Thomas H. Troeger

OXFORD
UNIVERSITY PRESS

Oxford University Press

Oxford   New York
Athens   Auckland   Bangkok   Bogotá   Buenos Aires   Cape Town
Chennai   Dar es Salaam   Delhi   Florence   Hong Kong   Istanbul   Karachi
Kolkata   Kuala Lumpur   Madrid   Melbourne   Mexico City   Mumbai   Nairobi
Paris   São Paulo   Singapore   Taipei   Tokyo   Toronto   Warsaw

with associated companies in   Berlin   Ibadan

Published by Oxford University Press, Inc.
198 Madison Avenue, New York, New York 10016

Oxford is a registered trademark of Oxford University Press

Library of Congress Cataloging-in-Publication Data
Troeger, Thomas H., 1945–
Above the Moon Earth Rises:
Hymn texts, anthems, and poems for a new creation
p. cm.
Includes indexes
ISBN 0-19-386419-3 (pbk.: alk paper)
1. Hymns, English. 2. Prayer. 3. Christian poetry.
I. Title
BV459 .T76 2001
264'.23—dc21   2001021500

1 3 5 7 9 8 6 4 2

Printed in the United States of America
on acid-free paper

for M. M.

By mortal love our hearts are drawn
to love's eternal spring . . .

Preface

This collection of hymns and anthems, rooted in Christian conviction, is intermixed with poems that do not draw upon faith. I am trying to map the landscape of the heart that still rejoices in God yet lives in a world that is largely oblivious to the spiritual dimension of life. I hope that the juxtaposition of the two perspectives opens each to the other: faith to the world and the world to faith. I have attempted to organize the poems so that the tension between the two perspectives is mutually illuminating. I believe that to live gracefully with this tension is the mark of wisdom. Such an understanding may baffle the dogmatic mind, but it does not lie beyond the capacity of the poetic imagination. The imagination often holds together realities that are logically inconsistent yet dynamically coherent.

As in my first collection, *Borrowed Light*, I have included indexes according to meter, theme and image, Scripture, and first lines to help pastors, liturgists, and church musicians locate what they need.

Although several of the hymns and anthems have already been set to music, I hope more composers will find in these texts inspiration to create settings that help us sing our way into a new creation.

Thomas H. Troeger

Ralph E. and Norma E. Peck Professor
    of Preaching & Communications
Iliff School of Theology
Denver, Colorado

Epiphany, 2000

Acknowledgements

I am grateful to the churches, institutions, schools, and individuals who commissioned many of the hymns and anthems in this collection. I find the Spirit of the living God working through their desire for new language to express their faith.

Here is a list of the commissioners and the hymn or anthem that I created for them in the order they appear in this collection: Shallowford Presbyterian Church, near Winston-Salem, North Carolina, in honor of their pastor David Partington: "God Saw that Earth Was Good." Timothy Edwards of the United Methodist Publishing House, a hymn for children: "How Bright the Dawn, the Sun's First Ray." The First United Unitarian Church of Dallas: "Each Breath Is Borrowed Air." The Second Presbyterian Church of Little Rock, Arkansas, in honor of their retiring minister of music, Rosella Duerksen: "Sing to God as Sings the Ocean." The First Presbyterian Church, Hartsville, South Carolina, for their sacred arts festival: "The Crickets Chanting through the Night." The Presbyterian Association of Musicians for the 100th anniversary of the Montreat Conference Center, North Carolina: "By Mortal Love Our Hearts Are Drawn." Friends of the Rev. James B. Lemler, an Episcopal priest, in honor of his ministry: "Love Simple Things to Train the Heart." The Denver Gay Men's Chorus: "Seeded in the Stars." Sally Ann Morris: "God Weeps with Us Who Weep and Mourn." Brookings United Church of Christ in Brookings, South Dakota, to celebrate their new church building: "Traveler, Are You Passing Through?" The Episcopal Church in the U.S.A. for its General Convention 2000: "Come to the Mountain." The Presbyterian Church of Cooperstown, New York, in memory of Kitty Ketchem and to celebrate their 200th anniversary: "Come Join Us as We Journey." The North American Academy of Liturgy to provide a hymn that people from many faith traditions could sing: "From Many Different Ancient Springs." Carlton Young: "Welcome, Welcome! The Door Is Open." The Presbyterian Association of Musicians for its annual conference at Westminster College: "Through Our Beating Hearts Remind Us." Virginia F. Gada in honor of her mother, Ruth Cole Fleshman, a great teacher and lover of education: "Thanks Be to God for Teachers." Sandy Cain in memory of her husband Ed Cain: "Safe Landing on a Distant Shore." Friends of Don Armitage for his ministry of music: "For God Risk Everything." Shadyside Presbyterian Church, Pittsburgh, to celebrate their past and to renew their vision: "We Live in that Far Future." The Roman Catholic Diocese of Ogdensburg, New York, to celebrate their 125th anniversary: "God Whose Word from Age to Age." Christ Episcopal Church in Rochdale, Massachusetts: "Christ Still Walks These Wooded Hills." The Chautauqua Institute for its 75th anniversary: "The

Seed that Cleaves a Stone." The First Presbyterian Church of the Covenant in Erie, Pennsylvania, to celebrate the past and look to the future: "Where the Cross Still Casts Its Shadow." The Rev. Clifford Johnson to celebrate his ministry upon retiring: "We Have Met Christ Raised and Living." St. John's Episcopal Cathedral in Denver in honor of the music ministry of Donald Pearson: "How Much We Owe to Those Who Live." First Presbyterian Church, Tallahassee, Florida, in honor of the Rev. Brant S. Copeland's 15th anniversary as pastor: "Look Who Gathers at Christ's Table." Chautauqua Institute in honor of the presidency of Dan Bratton: "Like Stars Positioned Far Apart." Mark Konewko for the beginning of school and for Catholic Schools Week: "We Look Down Deep to Look Out Far."

I am also indebted to Kimberly Dickerson, my student assistant, and to the many church musicians, pastors, and lay people who send me encouraging letters and e-mails about texts from my first volume, *Borrowed Light,* which they have sung or used in sermons and prayer groups. I am grateful as well to the following composers who have encouraged me to write by setting my poems as hymns, anthems, art songs, and larger choral works: René Clausen, Jonathan Crutchfield, Carol Doran, Brock Downward, Alfred Fedak, Richard Jeffrey, John Kuzma, Libby Larsen, Sally Ann Morris, Barry Oliver, Alice Parker, Donald Pearson, Walter Pelz, Richard Proulx, Carey Ratcliff, William Rowan, and Glenn Rudolph.

Iliff School of Theology and St. John's Episcopal Cathedral in Denver have each played a significant role in inspiring and support-ing my creative work. I am grateful for the way they feed both my heart and mind.

I especially want to recognize my wife, Merle Marie, to whom the collection is dedicated and who helped to gather these texts together from many different disks when chaos threatened to take over.

Contents

EARTH RISES

1 | Above the Moon Earth Rises

Above the moon earth rises,
a sunlit mossy stone,
a garden that God prizes
where life has richly grown,
an emerald selected
for us to guard with care,
an isle in space protected
by one thin reef of air.

The mossy stone is grieving,
its tears are bitter rain,
the garden is unleaving
and all its harvests wane,
the emerald is clouded,
its luster dims and fades,
the isle of life is shrouded
in thick and stagnant haze.

O listen to the sighing
of water, sky, and land
and hear the Spirit crying
the future is at hand.
The moss and garden thinning
portend a death or birth,
the end or new beginning
for all that live on earth.

A death if hearts now harden,
a birth if we repent
and tend and keep the garden
as God has always meant:
to sow without abusing
the soil where life is grown,
to reap without our bruising
this sunlit mossy stone.

2 | God Saw that Earth Was Good

God saw that earth was good
and with a joyful eye
observed how spring attires the wood
and clouds adorn the sky,
how water smoothes a stone
and light suffuses air
and yet God felt, oh, so alone,
and hungered for a prayer.

God loved the bird's bright song,
the ocean's beat and roar,
but hearing these would make God long
to hear still something more:
a word of shared delight
to see the rising sun,
to marvel at the stars by night
and count them one by one.

God scooped and shaped from earth
companions who would thrill
to see the beauty brought to birth
by their creator's will.
At their first word of praise
God's spirit danced and leapt,
but when they turned to brutal ways
God's spirit mourned and wept.

God, make our lives the prayer
your lonely spirit sought,
when longing for new friends to share
the beauty you had wrought,
you bravely dared to trust
your richest hopes and dreams
to creatures whom you made from dust
and fed with living streams.

3 | Aspen at Dusk

The clouds are leaving
but the mountains are staying—
although
from the beginning of dusk
they have tried on the same robes,
first gold, then rust,
fooling my eye
so I could not tell
which is rock and which is sky.

But now
over the mountains
one last cloud
thins to a wisp,
proving rock endures
past vapor and mist—
although
after ages and ages
of snow and rain
the clouds will gather here
over a plain.

4 | How Bright the Dawn, the Sun's First Ray

How bright the dawn, the sun's first ray
that marks the end of night!
For all day long, each time we pray
God sends more love and light.

From dawn to dusk praise God in song,
tell all that God has done:
God gives us breath and makes us strong
and warms the earth with sun.

God comes in Christ to show us how
we each can day by day
love one another here and now
and live the words we pray.

BORROWED AIR

5 | Each Breath is Borrowed Air

Each breath is borrowed air,
not ours to keep and own,
and all our breaths as one declare
what wisdom long has known:

to live is to receive
and answer back with praise
to what our minds cannot conceive:
the source of all our days.

The sea flows in our veins.
The dust of stars is spun
to form the coiled, encoded skeins
by which our cells are run:

to live is to receive
and answer back with praise
to what our minds cannot conceive:
the source of all our days.

From earth and sea and dust
arise yet greater things,
the wonders born of love and trust,
a grateful heart that sings:

to live is to receive
and answer back with praise
to what our minds cannot conceive:
the source of all our days.

And when our death draws near
and tries to dim our song,
our parting prayers will make it clear
to whom we still belong:

to live is to receive
and answer back with praise
to what our minds cannot conceive:
the source of all our days.

6 | Wind over the Plain

Wind over the plain:
wheat and grasses bending.
Wind upon the sea:
waves swelling and breaking.
Wind whistling through the forest:
trees bending and swaying.
Wind sweeping the desert:
dunes shifting and moving.
Wind buffing the ice fields:
snow swirling and drifting.
Wind shaking the rushes:
seeds floating and dancing.
Wind rushing through the canyon:
stone whistling and moaning.
Wind moving in and out of your lungs:
breath rising and falling.
The world alive with wind.
The world alive with breath.
The world alive with Spirit.
Windbreathspirit,
come!

7 | What Wind Would Carry?
(With a gift of flowers for one far away)

What wind would carry
the heavy seeds
of a sunflower
a thousand miles
and drop them down
in a welcoming place
to bloom again
with a golden crown
and a rich brown face?

Would the wind be a gale
from the vast wild seas?
No.
The strongest storms fail
when they meet the stubborn hills
and the stoutest trees.
Then,
what is the source
of a wind with the strength
to bear heavy seeds
half a continent's length?

Picture a couple,
though now far apart,
together,
looking at flowers
that reach for the skies
and trace the petals' reflection
in their delighted eyes,
and you will hear
a whisper of breath
that blows steadier
than the fiercest storm you've known,
and on that wind
look, look!
across half a continent
the heavy seeds are blown.

8 | I Love a Hint of Winter

I love a hint of winter—
when winter's far away—
the shadow of a dark cloud
that chills a summer day,
the sudden wind that blows,
thunder in the air,
then the memory of snows
and the maple gaunt and bare—
as if the sky announces:
warmth will never hold,
prepare the flesh and earth
for the coming, bitter cold.
And then the high hot sun
quickly shines again—
yet fails to melt the drifts
that are piling up within.

ANGELS VISIT

9 | Angels Visit when We Sing

Angels visit when we sing
and the morning stars rejoice,
we can hear them echoing
in each faithful heart and voice:

Alleluia, Alleluia!
Alleluia, Alleluia!

Angels visit when we sing
as they did at Jesus' birth
and the music that they bring
links the heavens with the earth:

Alleluia, Alleluia!
Alleluia, Alleluia!

Angels visit when we sing
and remind us with their praise
sin and death have lost their sting
for the crucified is raised:

Alleluia, Alleluia!
Alleluia, Alleluia!

Angels visit when we sing
and our hearts are touched by fire
as our hymns and anthems ring
with the sound of heaven's choir:

Alleluia, Alleluia!
Alleluia, Alleluia!

10 | Sing to God as Sings the Ocean

Sing to God as sings the ocean,
sing as birds that greet the dawn,
sing as windswept trees in motion,
sing and let your song be drawn
from God's vast and whole creation,
from your faith and doubt and fears,
from rebirth and re-creation,
from life's wealth of joy and tears.

Sing the heart's deep sighing sorrow
to the Lord who hears lament,
who at midnight sees tomorrow
when the dark at last is spent.
Sing to God who in our sadness
brings the news of coming light,
ample hope to waken gladness
and sustain us through the night.

Sing the great, glad joy of Jesus!
Sing the gospel that Christ brings.
Sing the way Christ heals and feeds us
Sing the song that Easter sings:
Christ is risen, Christ is living,
Christ among us, Christ within,
Christ the spring of endless giving
where new songs of faith begin.

11 | The Crickets Chanting through the Night

The crickets chanting through the night,
the windswept, whistling trees,
the birds that welcome morning light,
the humming, roaring seas
are each assigned the notes they sing
while we make up our part
and fashion God an offering
through our creative art.

The budding wood, the flowered field,
the mountain robed in snow,
the burrow and the nest that shield
the beasts from winds that blow
are from the same inventive mind
that dared to set us free
to probe how nature is designed
and bring new worlds to be.

Created to create, we ask,
O God, before we start
that you will join us in our task
by moving in our heart
so everything that we create,
compose, produce, invent
will help the earth to celebrate
and honor your intent.

BY MORTAL LOVE

12 | By Mortal Love
Our Hearts Are Drawn

By mortal love our hearts are drawn
to love's eternal spring:
the love that creatures greet at dawn,
the love that sparrows sing,
the love that feeds an infant's trust,
the love that nurtures ours,
the love that blesses our frail dust
with love's redemptive powers,

the love our violent world rejects
and fear and hatred scorn,
the love that each of us neglects
when weighted down and worn,
the love that even then persists
and nudges us with grace
as gentle as the morning mists
that wreathe this hallowed place,

as constant as the waterfall
cascading from the pond
that echoes love's profounder call
till we in love respond
and set the wooded mountainside
to ringing with our praise:
the spring of love we crucified
eternal love has raised!

13 | Love is a Thin Flame

Love is a thin flame,
a feather of gold
that waves in the night wind
against the vast cold,
you cup it with your hand
against sudden gales
but the wind whips around
and the flame sputters and fails.

What do you do
when you dreamed
of one room in two hearts
where the same faith lives
and the same hope starts?

What do you do
when you both come to know
there are rooms in each heart
where the other can't go?

14 | Love Simple Things to Train the Heart

Love simple things to train the heart
in love's profounder ways:
the sun at dawn, the buds that start
at spring's less slanted rays,
the signs in sky and land and sea,
in fields and leafy wood
of God who brought all things to be
and then pronounced them good.

Then love a child, a neighbor, friend,
a stranger new to town,
an enemy you would expend
except that you have found
the word made flesh in every face,
the Christ who comes to you
and gives your heart sufficient grace
to love as he would do.

Attend to how the wind draws song
from trees that bend and sway,
reminding us we all belong
to whom we bow and pray:
the deep and wordless sighing breath
that animates our dust
and even in the face of death
still wakens love and trust.

O Love, whose love for love has spun
the earth, the sea, the skies,
who dwells as Christ in everyone,
and prays through our deep sighs,
transfigure by your trinity
the patterns of our love
till in our actions all can see
your Light and Life and Dove.

15 | Seeded in the Stars

In the beginning,
in a time before time,
in a space before space,
a cloud of dust
gathered and compacted
until it burst
in a shower of stars,
unnumbered configurations
of matter and light
dancing, dancing,
dancing through the night
and filling our dreams
like the leaves of a boundless forest
shaken by a gale
with every leaf
swirling, swirling,
swirling down.

Can you name the pattern
they will form on the ground?
Name it now
while they're still
swirling, swirling,
swirling down?

Can you predict which thumb
of which maple leaf
will lock with the forefinger
of a hickory leaf beside it?
Can you plot the way
the leaves will all nuzzle
when they've taken their places
in the forest floor puzzle?

Can you name it now
while they're still
swirling, swirling,
swirling down?

If a forest
from year to year
never fills
with the same mosaic of fallen leaves
it should be no surprise
that we creatures of stardust
are as varied
as the configurations of the skies
and prismatic as their light,
not divided by halves and by twos,
but an infinite gradation
of infinite hues,
each flowing into the next
as the river flows to the ocean
that sends up the cloud
that brings down the rain
that fills up the streams
that feed the lake
that empties into the river
that flows to the ocean,
one element
in unceasing motion
that is no less water
when it flows in the river
than when it swells as the tide,
like the lift of love
that is no less love
when it flows from man to man
than when it shines
in the face of a bride.

Suddenly!
a fierce wind
disrupts the dance of

dust and star,
leaf and light,
water and love
and on the wind
shrill voices cry:
faggot, fairy,
pervert, sissy, queer,
deviant, stranger,
the utterly other
though sharing
the same star dust
we are sister and brother
whose hearts take their beat
from the start of all things,
from the pulse of the dance
that we join as we chant
a chorus of names
to still the fierce wind:
we are shaman, healer, magicmaker,
clairvoyant, mediator, seer,
artist and priest,
lover and friend,
the litany never ends,
but runs on through the dance
with a wild, exuberant gladness
at the wealth of love's ways,
and the knowledge
that no single love
is ideal and best
except the love that trusts
that all love is blest,
blest by the dance of dust and star,
leaf and light,
water and love
and the riches
our histories hold,
of all kinds of people
who have lived and loved
age after age

and given us art and beauty,
song and dance,
knowledge and wisdom
beyond what we can gauge
though we still hear their song
and we still dance their dance,
swirling, swirling, swirling,
singing, singing, singing

singing as the avatars
of the multiplicitous stars,
glad that the dust of cosmic storms
finds in our life and love
so many varied forms,

singing as the leaves
of the vast wood,
glad to swirl in patterns
unpredictable
but beautiful and good,

singing as the gradations
of the prism's angled beams,
glad to reveal love's light
is a spectrum of dreams,

singing as the water
spilling from the sky
and rushing to the sea,
glad that levee and dam
cannot control
what kind of element
we will be,

singing as the current of love
that flows
from man to man,
glad that our passion and fire
were seeded in the stars
when all things began.

16 | Jesu, Jesu

Jesu, Jesu,
Hallelujah!
We praise you, praise you,
Hallelujah!

Precious king,
come riding!
Come riding through town,
no purple robe and no golden crown,
no palace, no court
but the folk in the street
who sing Hallelujah
and fall at your feet.

Jesu, Jesu,
Hallelujah!
We praise you, praise you,
Hallelujah!

Precious king,
keep riding!
Keep riding, dear Lord,
no mighty armies, no iron sword,
no chariot, no horse
but a donkey and palms
and glad Hallelujahs,
wild cheering and psalms.

Jesu, Jesu,
Hallelujah!
We praise you, praise you,
Hallelujah!

Precious king,
keep riding!
Keep riding on by,
ride down our streets and ride up the sky.
We'll beat on our drum,
and your donkey will prance.
To glad Hallelujahs
we'll leap and we'll dance.

Jesu, Jesu,
Hallelujah!
We praise you, praise you,
Hallelujah!

17 | With Holy Anger, Christ

With holy anger, Christ,
disrupt the power that feeds
upon the cruel sacrifice
of others' rights and needs.
As you turned over tables
and sent coins
spinning and jangling
across the temple floor,
disrupt the unholy commerce
in our hearts:
selling faith
for security
and trading justice
for peace.

By your holy anger
drive out every transaction
that profanes
the house of prayer.

By that same anger start
what evil can't defeat:
a stubborn passion in the heart
to see God's will complete.
Baptize us with fire
hotter than Herod's wrath
until we no longer mute
the fury in our hearts
at the slaughter
of the innocents.
Baptize us with fire!
But do not let our rage
grow bitter as the din
of fierce mean minds that fail to gauge
when anger turns to sin.

Instead, let anger be
the first note
in love's ascending scale,
the starting tone
of heaven's dove:
"O Jerusalem, Jerusalem,
if only you knew
the things that make for peace . . ."
Instead, let anger be
compassion's kindling fire
that lights in us the energy
to live as you desire.

18 | Yes, I Know We Both Agreed

Yes, I know we both agreed,
"It's an extravagance," and
then you said, "Nothing more.
There's not a thing that I need.
Not one thing more."

So take this one little, extra gift
not for your need but mine:
my need to love and adore,
my need for a token and sign
of what this day means to me:
that when you were born
there came a little girl whose grace—
like her mother's—
would ripen and grow
till she became the wisest and kindest soul
I would ever know.

And if you still find it extravagant,
think on this:
you gave me yourself
for as long as we live
("till death do us part"
as the old service said).
So take and enjoy
the gift that I give
and by your receiving
feed the need of my heart
to mark this day with a sacrament
that brims over with the riches that remain
when my best words are spent.

19 | Let Jove Rise from His Couch of Clouds

Let Jove rise from his couch of clouds
filtering the light upon the Aegean sea,
and let him carouse
unfettered by age and mortality,
seeking Athena or any goddess attired
in enough gauze and gold
to awaken his flesh-like fleshless desire,
never dimmed by growing old,
and grant him yet one more rush of delight,
but then lead him to look into the eyes
of my beloved, and if divine knowledge is keen as
    human sight,
he will abandon the skies
and pray to live on earth,
risking mortal pulse and mortal death
and every stress that follows mortal birth
to know what I know with every breath:
eternity is not forever young and new,
eternity is the grace I have known through you,
a beauty of heart, a beauty of soul,
a beauty only hinted by the beauty of gold,
but since the heart craves a material sign, a tangible
    thing,
I hope when you wear this, your heart will sing.

BORN IN A BARN

20 | Born in a Barn where Cows and Sheep

Born in a barn where cows and sheep
huddle in the frosty air,
Mary's baby falls asleep
while she lifts her heart in prayer:

Thanks be to God for friendly beasts
that tonight have not been fed
so my newborn child at least
has a manger for his bed.

Out in the dark while cattle low
Mary hears another sound:
through the streets the soldiers go,
Herod's troops patrol the town.

Quick with her hand she shades the light
till the boot steps fade away,
but they haunt her dreams all night
and keep waking her to pray:

Deep in the soul let starlight spring,
make each heart a manger stall
till we live what angels sing:
Peace on earth, good will to all!

21 | Disturbed by Light

Disturbed by light
while fighting sleep,
their eyes half closed,
half watching sheep,
the shepherds might
have turned away
and rested till the break of day:

Why risk the night,
the winds that blow?
Why risk the way
we do not know?

Disturbed by light
that marked the sky
where dark alone
once met the eye,
the magi might
have paused to test
the wisdom of their star-born quest:

Why risk the night,
the winds that blow?
Why risk the way
we do not know?

Disturbed by light
that draws us past
the world we grip
so hard and fast,
we might delay
our starting out
until we answer every doubt:

Why risk the night,
the winds that blow?
Why risk the way
we do not know?
except—
except our hearts
refuse to slow
and every beat insists we go.

22 | Angel and Star

Angel and star,
music and light:
gifts for the child
born in the night.

Sing with the choir,
greeting the birth.
Deepen their song,
live it on earth.

Shine with the star,
send out its ray.
In the deep dark
brighten the way.

Sing with the choir,
gladden the night.
Shine with the star,
point to the light.

23 | Cameo Angel

An angel carved from seashell
has made its way
up from the deep
on the tide's full swell
and from imaginings
of ancient messengers
with feather down wings
that fluttered back and forth
from heaven's sky
to the carver's hand
and the carver's eye

with the same dance of delight
that lifted my heart
to dream of you
receiving an angel
on Christmas day
to announce without words
what words cannot say.

24 | Are You a Shepherd?
(Christmas Pageant)

Are you a shepherd
startled by light,
hearing the heavens
singing at night?

Whatever part
you play in the story,
God grant you a heart
open to glory!

Are you an angel
holding the star,
guiding the magi
traveling afar?

Whatever part . . .

Are you attending
Christ sound asleep,
Mary the mother
hushing the sheep?

Whatever part . . .

Or are you Joseph
weary and worn,
fearing the slaughter
Herod has sworn?

Whatever part . . .

Are you a traveler
not here to stay,
taking your journey
home a new way?

Whatever part . . .

25 | One Gift the Magi Bore

One gift the magi bore
worth more than all the rest:
the grace to kneel and bow before
the child whom starlight blest.

Their myrrh and frankincense
lay sweet upon the air,
but sweeter yet and more intense
the magi's humble prayer.

And though their gift of gold
shone brightly with the skies
still heaven's light was twice as bold
in their adoring eyes.

One gift the magi bore
worth more than all the rest:
we give that gift when we adore
the child whom starlight blest.

26 | Directions for Magi

Be constant as the star
that guides you from above.
The trip is strenuous and far
that leads from fear to love.

When snow that drives and drifts
has blocked the sky from view,
take shelter till the blizzard lifts,
the star will wait for you.

The light that bright star sends
at last will come to rest,
revealing where the journey ends
begins a deeper quest.

GOD WEEPS

27 | God Weeps with Us
   Who Weep and Mourn

God weeps with us who weep and mourn,
God's tears flow down with ours,
and God's own heart is bruised and worn
from all the heavy hours
of watching while the soul's bright fire
burned lower day by day,
and pulse and breath and love's desire
dimmed down to ash and clay.

Through tears and sorrow, God, we share
a sense of your vast grief:
the weight of bearing every prayer
for healing and relief,
the burden of our questions why,
the doubts that they engage,
and as our friends and lovers die,
our hopelessness and rage.

And yet because, like us, you weep,
we trust you will receive
and in your tender heart will keep
the ones for whom we grieve
while with your tears our hearts will taste
the deep dear core of things
from which both life and death are graced
by love's renewing springs.

28 | Cradle Lament

My little one crying,
in eighty years
the old one dying,
and I by then
no longer replying.

29 | Come in Silence, Named but Nameless

Come in silence, named but nameless.
Come in silence, living flame.
Quiet all our pious babble
and through silence speak your name.
By your silence set our hearts to weeping
for the sin and harm of facile preaching
that misused your word and teaching
to suppress the dreams you stirred

in the slaves who sought their freedom,
in the women who rebelled,
in the science that discovered
what the Bible does not tell,
in the mind's incessant, restless sounding
of elusive truth, complex, confounding,
in new theories whose propounding
threatened ancient creeds and laws.

We confess our own swift judgments
and the harm and wrong we do
when our fears and hates projected
claim to be a word from you.
Let us rightly use your name in speaking
to affirm that all are in your keeping
while we never cease from seeking
ways to welcome your new light.

PASSING THROUGH

30 | Traveler, Are You Passing Through?

Traveler, are you passing through?
We are on a journey too.
Here we meet to feast and rest,
cach of us, likc you, a gucst.
We have found a deep spring here,
constant water, pure and clear,
and a fire to keep us warm
through the night, the cold and storm.

Traveler, have you lost your way?
We have room for you to stay.
Come on in and spend the night.
Wait until the morning light.
Tell us where you started from,
where you've been, how far you've come.
We will tell what we have learned:
where we doubled back and turned.

Traveler, have you far to go?
Up ahead is hard and slow.
At our table take a seat.
We have more than we can eat.
Join us and renew your strength
needed for the journey's length.
You, our guest, be host instead.
Bless and break and pass the bread.

Traveler, have we met before?
Sharing bread we share far more,
share our stories, songs, and prayers,
share our common hopes and cares
till it dawns on us to trace
in your eyes and in your face
what we sensed but hardly knew:
Christ our friend is here in you!

31 | We're Sailing, We're Sailing

We're sailing, we're sailing
out from the strand
just past the reef
to an island of sand.

We'll count every star
that shines in the skies
till they're stolen by dawn
and the wind starts to rise.

We'll push off at once
and we won't look back
at the dunes and the beach
that the storms will attack.

Reclaimed by the sea,
and marked on no chart
the island of sand
will be fixed in our heart.

32 | Come with Moses to the Mountain

Come with Moses to the mountain,
stand before the bush in flame,
where the very ground is holy
and the Spirit calls your name.
Then return and take the vision
that has blazed upon this height
to the church and world that hunger
for its liberating light.

Come with Jesus to the mountain
where, transfigured, he transforms
hearts that stumble in the shadows
cast by life's persistent storms.
Strengthened by the light and glory
that have crowned the summit's slope
hasten homeward with the vision
to rebuild the church with hope.

Come rejoicing to the mountain,
to the highest, holy height
where the love of God and neighbor
is your first and chief delight,
where the flame that dazzled Moses
and the brightness of Christ's face
will create a new creation
of eternal love and grace.

33 | Come to the Mountain
(A mini-oratorio for church choir and congregation)

I. Prelude

[lament: choir and/or soloists]

Where Moses leads his flock
upon the mountainside,
the sound of bleating lambs
tumbles up and down the rock
bleating, bleating, bleating,
and loosens in his heart
the echo of his people
weeping, weeping, weeping
for the burden that they bear:
grief their only hymn,
lament their only prayer,
weeping, weeping, weeping . . .

Fire
roars
through the branches of a bush
with intensities of light
that make the desert sun
seem a dying coal,
yet not one twig,
not one leaf
of the burning bush
curls to ash in the tongues of flame.

Silent falls the weeping heart,
silent falls the bleating lamb,
silent at the words that start,
"I the Lord, I AM, I AM."

[congregation and choir]

Come with Moses to the mountain,
stand before the bush in flame,
where the very ground is holy
and the Spirit calls your name.
Then return and take the vision
that has blazed upon this height
to the church and world that hunger
for its liberating light.

II. Offertory

[pilgrimage song: choir and/or soloists]

Where Jesus climbs
his close friends follow.
Step by step Christ leads the way.
At every turn
his friends stop
and look upward
to see how far they have to go.
Step by step Christ leads the way.
Again they start.
Again they stop.
Again they raise their eyes.
Step by step Christ leads the way.
Again they start.
Again they stop.
Again they raise their eyes . . .

[theophany: choir and/or soloists]

Christ commands the summit's height!
His robes, his face transformed by light!
Moses and Elijah appear.
A cloud casts upon the peak
a shadow of light instead of shade:
"This is my beloved son.
Listen to him."
Cloud and prophets vanish.
The friends see
no one but only Jesus,
but only Jesus,
only Jesus,
Jesus.

Come with Jesus to the mountain
where, transfigured, he transforms
hearts that stumble in the shadows
cast by life's persistent storms.
Strengthened by the light and glory
that have crowned the summit's slope
hasten homeward with the vision
to rebuild the church with hope.

III. Postlude

[pastoral and vision song: choir and/or soloists]

The wolf and the lamb
graze in the pasture,
the ox and the lion
feed at one trough,
while the blacksmith's hammer,
metal on metal
ringing and singing,
beats swords into plowshares,
ringing and singing
beats spears into pruning hooks,
ringing and singing
beats guns into girders,
ringing and singing
beats tanks into tractors,
ringing and singing
till the sound becomes the song
of all people on earth
who stream to the mountain of God
to learn the way of the Lord.

They shall not hurt or destroy
in all my holy mountain.
Blood shall no more darken the soil,
no more cry out from the ground.
No more shall a weeping earth
weep to a weeping heaven.
They shall not hurt or destroy
in all my holy mountain.

[congregation and choir]

Come rejoicing to the mountain,
to the highest, holy height
where the love of God and neighbor
is your first and chief delight,
where the flame that dazzled Moses
and the brightness of Christ's face
will create a new creation
of eternal love and grace.

34 | Come, Join Us as We Journey

Come, join us as we journey
beyond what we have known.
All seeking hearts are welcome.
No need to go alone.
For there are shadowed valleys
and mountains, high and steep,
and many river crossings
with currents swift and deep.

A solitary traveler
by night or even day
discouraged and exhausted
can easily lose the way.
We need each other's wisdom,
each other's care and strength
to make the whole great journey,
its full and winding length.

Sometimes we travel singing,
sometimes in tears and grief,
sometimes our hearts will struggle
with doubt and disbelief,
sometimes with hope and passion
our faith will burn so bright
that we will boldly travel
though starless be the night.

We are not in a hurry.
We're called to stop and serve
whatever needs may greet us
round every peak and curve.
We work toward peace through justice,
and where the road ascends
we catch anew the vision
of what our God intends.

We sometimes pass a marker
of those long gone from sight:
a work of love and kindness
that still reflects the light
that beckoned them to journey
beyond what they had known,
and then we pray our witness
may shine as theirs has shone.

And oftentimes a stranger
will join us as we go,
someone who knows us better
than we ourselves can know,
who sits with us at supper
and prays and breaks the bread
then vanishing yet calls us
to journey on ahead.

35 | The Land Promises
More to the Eye

The land promises more to the eye
than the land gives.

The cedars at the end of the field,
just on the other side of the stone wall,
snag the last scraps of dusk.
Now gold,
now coal,
the topmost boughs
draw my sight toward the distant peak.

One fading cloud hovers
a hop, skip, and a jump
past the summit,
and from there it seems
an easy walk to heaven
except
the sun sets faster than the heart can run
and there is a moment—
oh, such a long, long moment—
before the eye can see the stars
that mark the final stretch.

Or is it that the stars hesitate
to come out
and spend their light
as foolishly
as the dying day?

What I see is:
the end of the field,
the stone fence,
the cedars,
their topmost boughs,
the peak,
the cloud
are all gone—
except in the re-adjusted light
of the modest stars
I see a patch of snow on the summit
and remember
all that the land promised:
heaven,
a hop, skip, and a jump away—
now dissolved
into
night.

36 | From Many Different Ancient Springs

From many different ancient springs,
O God, your rivers flow
and bear a wealth of offerings
that feed our need to know
in clearer and profounder ways
how you—unseen, divine—
meet mortal flesh through prayer and praise,
through ritual, song and sign.

Flow on, flow on through the prayerful heart,
flow on, O source of all our streams,
flow on and flowing on impart
the life that renews our hopes and dreams.

We're humbled when we try to chart
each river's twisting course,
the subtle ways it shapes the heart
and bears from you its source
those meanings that elude the grasp
of all the thoughts we weave
when faithful to the scholar's task
we probe what we believe.

Flow on, flow on . . .

We gladly join with all who bring
the fruit your streams have fed:
the varied ways we pray and sing
and share in breaking bread,
the gift of grace that you have sown
that opens us to see
through forms of prayer unlike our own
prayer's rich complexity.

Flow on, flow on . . .

Far downstream, past the final bend,
dear friends have gone from sight
whom we by prayer with thanks commend
to your transforming light
that shone through their own lives of prayer
and made their work and play
refractions of your love and care
that never pass away.

Flow on, flow on . . .

Although we part, we still are bound
by gifts that you bestow.
From depths that we have yet to sound,
new truth and visions flow
that sweep us past the present shore
and bear us on to greet
with great glad thanks the holy roar
where all your rivers meet.

Flow on, flow on . . .

37 | Somewhere I Have Never Traveled

Somewhere I have never traveled
is the place I long to be—
its hills, its plains, and streams
are known yet unknown to me—
just beyond the last vision of my waking dreams,
over the edge of the mind's vast sea
and still past that to a farther rim—
there, precisely there,
marked on no map or chart
but glimpsed through hope,
through the reach and the stretch of the yearning heart
and the wordless prayer it offers
when the land I've walked
and the silhouette of the hills
against the last leaning light of day
are carried off in the rising breath
of wind blowing through the darkened cedars
that sway and bow to the music
sounding from somewhere I have never traveled.

38 | Welcome, Welcome! The Door is Open

Welcome, welcome! The door is open,
there's room for all who come,
the table's laid, the meal prepared,
enough for everyone.

This is God's feast,
unlike any other,
where the greatest and least
are sister and brother.

Welcome, welcome! You're not too early,
too late, too well-to-do,
too poor to be an honored guest.
A place is set for you.

This is God's feast,
unlike any other,
where the greatest and least
are sister and brother.

Welcome, welcome! come join the circle.
Enjoy the wine and bread,
and pass them on to foes and friends
till everyone is fed.

This is God's feast,
unlike any other
where the greatest and least
are sister and brother.

THROUGH OUR
BEATING HEARTS

39 | Through Our Beating Hearts Remind Us

Through our beating hearts remind us
that the source of all our powers
is, O God, your vital Spirit
that is animating ours.
Every pulse beat is revealing
while we work and while we rest
that your care for us is constant
and to live is to be blest.

Yet we act as if our living
were our own accomplishment
and the purpose of creation
is whatever we invent.
We ignore the truth repeated
every second by our hearts:
that our thanks should be unending
for the life your life imparts.

Brood and breathe on us your creatures
as you did upon the sea
when you split apart the darkness
and you called all things to be.
Brood and breathe and recreate us
till in Christ we are made new
and your never-ending giving
is returned through us to you.

40 | Thanks Be to God for Teachers

Infant child,
you gaze around
at all things new.
You babble, wail,
you smile and coo
and trust the world
will answer you.

Thanks be to God for teachers
who nurture what the child makes clear:
that learning springs from trust, not fear.

Little one,
you stand, you step,
you fall down boom.
You stand, you step,
you fall down boom.
You stand, you step,
you cross the room!

Thanks be to God for teachers
who trust the wisdom toddlers know:
we all fall down to learn and grow.

Playful child,
you run, you skip
you leap up high.
You flap yours arms,
you want to fly
and touch the stars
that fill the sky.

Thanks be to God for teachers
who help creative thinking spring
from children's wild imagining.

Searching youth,
you snap the ties
that childhood weaves,
the magic world
the eye perceives,
the simple creed the heart believes.

Thanks be to God for teachers
who honor what the youth attest:
that doubt as well as faith is blest.

Young adult,
you hope the good
your heart intends
survives the times
life's road descends
through tangled wood
to unmapped ends.

Thanks be to God for teachers,
who ready both the mind and heart
for worlds the present cannot chart.

Middle aged,
you live between
your children's cries
and parents' needs,
and when you rise
you pray that God
will make you wise.

Thanks be to God for teachers
who guide a soul in how to weigh
the dawn and dying of the day.

Rich in years,
your heart still leaps
at birds in flight
but now by faith
you stretch your sight
beyond the stars
that fill the night.

Thanks be to God for teachers
who by their lives this faith have sown:
one day we'll know as we are known.

41 | Obelisks, Stelae, Sculpted Sarcophagi

Obelisks, stelae, sculpted sarcophagi,
special-issue stamps,
three-day weekends,
sales on twenty-seven-inch TVs,
and vacuum cleaners
are the monuments of the birthday magnificos
who reigned or conquered
or obsessed a nation's soul,
but not one gaudy monument preserves
what we celebrate this day:
the pleasure of deep conversation,
a ski through pasture and woods,
laughter and tears
and a shared meal
with one we hold as dear as you.

So here is a gift too small
for any grand public place,
but ample enough to mark in the heart
how we give thanks
for your company,
your friendship and grace.

42 | Two Poems from Those Who Have Lost Language

Language gone,
crossed wires, crossed words, missed connections,
not even able to ask for a glass of water,
my mother,
looking out the window
from her raised bed:
"The sun is braided purple."

I think:
purple, like the bruise of memory.
My father, after his stroke,
when I had asked,
"Is the sky blue?"
answered: "No, I mean yes."
And then I asked:
"Is your name Henry?"
"No, I mean yes."
So I kept asking
all the while knowing
no meant yes
and yes meant no.
But I tired trying
to help him reconnect syllables,
till he broke my silence:
"Yes, No,
let's go."

And now his voice
for so long unheard
sounds in my mother's:
"The sun is braided purple."

I look at the setting sun
and observe,
"Oh, Mom, that's very poetic."
She says:
"No, I mean yes."

43 | It is Lonely

It is lonely
to be a newcomer among the dead.
For we are a tiny minority
among the unnumbered population
of the ages.
They ignore us,
fearful that we might remind them
of the loneliness
they suffered when they were newcomers,
then they would feel again
the burdens which they,
like us,
first brought here,
but which now are as forgotten
as the memory of their pulse.

It is lonely
to be a newcomer among the dead.
For all the newcomers
are still longing
for the living
whom they have left behind.

It is lonely
to be a newcomer among the dead.
For there are things
you want to tell earth,
but when you say this
to the ancient dead,
they ask:
"Earth? What is earth?"

They turn their backs to you,
and to prove them wrong
you cry out
with all your voice,
a cry louder than any cry
you ever made on earth,
but instead of hearing sound
you see in the distance
the faintest tracery of light,
a comet,
a meteor,
a filament of brightness,
rising and falling with your cry,
gone as quickly as it appeared.

Then you notice
there are other comets,
other meteors,
other filaments of brightness,
not in time with your own voice,
but random,
unbidden by you,
one after another,
each isolated and discrete.
You keep crying,
hoping that the trail of your cry
will intersect
the trail of another's.

You cry again and again,
and you mark
the disappearing path of every cry,
isolated, alone,
and fading into darkness,
until wearied by your efforts
you turn back
toward the ancient dead,
realizing
what you judged apathy
is wisdom:
the wisdom of withdrawing
from what you cannot alter,
the compassion of allowing the living
to do
what only the living can do.

44 | Safe Landing on a Distant Shore

Safe landing on a distant shore
begins by setting out
across the deep that holds in store
calm days and storms of doubt.

We sense in every gale and breeze
their generating force
that even in the wildest seas
directs our shifting course.

And when the darkest night descends
and not one star appears
Christ walks the shadowed turbulence
of our unfathomed fears.

Christ calls when mortal hope has died
to hope in one thing more:
that borne on love's eternal tide
we'll safely land ashore.

RISK EVERYTHING

45 | For God Risk Everything!

For God risk everything!
since everything we own,
our laughter, tears, the songs we sing,
our breath, our flesh and bone,
are no more ours to keep
than wind that rushes by
or dreams that flicker in our sleep
or clouds that fade to sky.

How shriveled, Lord, the soul
that grips what it receives
and dares not free its anxious hold
but foolishly believes
that you are too severe
to pardon any loss,
forgetting how your son made clear
forgiveness on the cross.

From hearts that hide and hoard
the treasures that you send,
free us, till we by faith, O Lord,
shall act as you intend,
till we risk all for you,
risk everything you give,
and risking learn what Jesus knew:
by risking all we live.

46 | To My Equestrian Friend

The only horse I'd dare to mount
is Pegasus,
who bounds the clouds
with clopless hoofs
and mythy wings
and never dumps a rider
into the world of
substantial things.

Yours the braver heart by far:
to guide the bit
between teeth
and swing into the saddle
and trust the four legs
of another creature
to read
a signal from your brain
shot through the synapse
of your knee and hand:
leap, land.

For you at sixteen
I offer this prayer:
be as brave in your dreams
as you are in the saddle
when you leap through the air.

47 | We Live in that Far Future

We live in that far future
our founders could not see,
that strange new world and culture
that time would bring to be,
yet God gave them a vision
and fed their prayer and praise
inspiring their decision
to build for future days.

And when we sing God's glory
and hear and do God's word
we pass along the story
that our own parents heard
and told to us confessing
how they themselves received
the gospel and its blessing
from parents who believed:

The Word that shaped creation
spans all of time and space
and greets each generation
with that same gift of grace
that brightened one small manger
where sheep and oxen fed
and welcomed every stranger
and served them wine and bread.

Though crucified, now living,
Christ is the Word we sing,
compassionate, forgiving,
whose love and presence bring
the grace to keep believing
that through our words and deeds
in ways past our conceiving
God plants the future's seeds.

The grain we sow for reaping
will ripen to the ear
while we in Christ are sleeping
and waiting till we hear
in one quick eyelid's flutter
the final trumpet call
when age to age shall utter
that God is all in all.

48 | The Bush in Flame but not Consumed

The bush in flame but not consumed
wakens our desire
to bring the truths we have assumed
before its searching fire,
and yet we find as we draw near
our steps begin to slow,
afraid of what the light makes clear
yet wanting still to know.

As Moses did not run away
from that revealing flame,
Lord, make us bold to stand this day
and bear your holy name
and claim our call and bow beneath
the hands that will ordain
our strength and thought, our pulse and breath
to help bring in your reign.

And when we meet resistant hearts
let us with grace recall
how long it took by fits and starts
for us to heed your call,
and through that knowledge build our trust
in your persistent powers
to nurture in our stubborn dust
faith's richest fruit and flowers.

49 | God, Whose Word from Age to Age

God, whose word from age to age
stirred the prophets' holy thunder
and the wisdom of the sage,
has revealed a greater wonder:

Christ tomorrow, Christ today,
is the same as yesterday,
circling every time and place
with eternal love and grace.

Christ, who came to bear our cares
at the time that God appointed,
has adopted us as heirs:
by the Spirit we're anointed!

Christ tomorrow, Christ today, . . .

Christ, who brought the poor good news,
preached the reign of God with passion,
healed the sick, and soothed the bruised,
calls to us to show compassion:

Christ tomorrow, Christ today, . . .

Christ unites all things again,
reconciles the world we shattered,
beckons home and welcomes in
all whom hate and fear have scattered.

Christ tomorrow, Christ today, . . .

Praise to Christ with every breath,
Christ whose love past comprehending
stands with us through birth and death,
Christ the start and Christ the ending.

Christ tomorrow, Christ today, . . .

Praise to Christ for all the years
he has made our churches leaven
as they drew this world of tears
closer to the reign of heaven.

Christ tomorrow, Christ today, . . .

50 | The Church under Reconstruction

Some said
there had been too much rain
and the roof
long cracked after years of stress
gave way from water seeping in

others said
what fell from the heavens
had nothing to do with it
that the earth had shifted
and the church walls
had pushed out toward the market
so that the massive mosaic icon
of the Almighty Father God
had fallen in and left
a hole
a silhouette of the figure
whose fierce eyes
once dominated the great domed ceiling

services now
were held under the God-shaped hole
prayers said
sermons preached
offerings made
hymns sung
infants baptized
couples wed
the dead remembered

meanwhile reconstruction began
but it turned out harder than planned

some folks had taken home
bits of the original mosaic
as a piece of devotion or historical curiosity
and once it was discovered
there was not enough left to restore
the original ancient grandeur
debates erupted if they should even try
to recreate what was lost

some said
they should begin and finish the project
as quickly as possible
because people were not coming as they used to
since the great domineering icon
had vanished

others pointed out
new people were entering the church
curious about the place
in a way they never were before

and these newcomers joined
with those who had always been scared
by the icon's fierce eyes
to suggest they replace the old image
with a new one

the differences about what to do
broke into conflict
so that for now the construction
was nearly halted
though some workers
tried to assemble the roof in bits and pieces

but without an overall plan
nothing would stay put
even the stars that surrounded the hole
began to fall from the ceiling
so that another party arose
suggesting they take down the entire
edifice and start all over anew

except that the most devout
could not bear to lose this or that altar
where they had prayed so long
and the stones were worn smooth
by the knees of many generations

so for the time being
all that was done
was to rope off the area beneath
the God-shaped hole
to make sure no one was hit by a piece of mosaic
that would fall from time to time
from a cracked angel or star
and to pray
that people would keep coming
while the church continued to be
as the sign alerting those who entered said
under reconstruction.

51 | Christ Still Walks
These Wooded Hills

Christ still walks these wooded hills
as he walked them in the days
when the workers from the mills
gathered in this house of praise,
where they shared Christ's wine and bread,
then went home through field and wood
giving thanks their hearts were fed
and their lives were understood.

Though the earth has long received
those who built these holy walls
yet we trust as they believed
in the living Christ who calls,
who invites us to this place
where the Spirit brings to view
how our mission can embrace
worlds our founders never knew.

Through the windows of the church
we can see the treetops toss
while inside we pray and search
for the strength to bear the cross,
there we meet a stronger gale
than the stoutest tree that bends,
wind whose strength will never fail
when we do what Christ intends.

52 | As the Seed that Cleaves a Stone

As the seed that cleaves a stone
when its stubborn roots unfurl,
faith digs down where it is sown,
cracking through our hardened world.
Yet faith needs the sun and rain
of the grace that God provides,
or it bears no fruit and grain
but instead withdraws and dies.

As the growth a seed imparts
far exceeds its pebbled size,
faith expands our narrow hearts
past the bounds our doubts surmise.
Yet without the living streams
that through art and science flow,
faith contracts its hopes and dreams
and it ceases then to grow.

Here we greet the sun and rain,
here the living streams run deep,
here we gather in the grain
from the harvest that we reap
when our faith and art and thought
find their center, Lord, in you
and in all that you have wrought
that is beautiful and true.

53 | Where the Cross Still Casts its Shadow

Where the cross still casts its shadow
there we trace love's depth and height
pouring forth to bless and hallow
our own lives with that same light
which through every twist and turning
of our church's early days
helped our founders in discerning
how to serve the God they praised.

Though they long ago have parted
from this rise of windswept shore
still the mission that they started
and the fruit their witness bore
beckon us to keep attending
to the Spirit's wind and flame
and the work that God's intending
we will do in Jesus' name:

Meeting needs that stretch our mission
past the world our founders knew
yet maintaining their tradition,
Gracious God, of serving you,
while our lives keep growing, reaching,
toward the light, the love that's fed
all our praying, singing, preaching:
Christ, the church's Lord and head.

54 | Put Out from Shore to Cast Your Nets

Put out from shore to cast your nets
as deep and wide and far
as God whose web of love connects
the earth to every star.

Each sandy beach, each shallow bay,
each shoal in Galilee
was known by those Christ called away
to fish a vaster sea.

Put out from shore to cast your nets . . .

Our founders fished these circling shores
and farmed these rolling hills
and hallowed here their daily chores
by seeking what God wills.

Put out from shore to cast your nets . . .

Through word and deed, through sharing bread,
through hearts that welcome all,
through justice done, God's reign will spread
and sound again Christ's call.

Put out from shore to cast your nets . . .

Christ, let no line of rocky beach,
no sweep of rising land
constrain this church's stretch and reach
to live what you command.

Put out from shore to cast your nets . . .

Then shall our heirs in future days
give thanks for what we dared,
and when they gather for God's praise
hear you, O Christ, declare:

Put out from shore to cast your nets . . .

55 | Like Stars Positioned Far Apart

Like stars positioned far apart
across the skies of night,
too often science, faith, and art
are points of single light
whose powers do not congregate
to burn the dark away
but shining lone and isolate
ignore each other's ray.

And yet, O God, in you exist
whatever things that are,
and by your will they all persist:
the dark, the light, the star,
the cells from which our thoughts are knit,
our science, prayer, and art—
for all their differences they fit
in your expansive heart.

Grant us a mind more like your mind,
as ample as the skies
where truth that we have yet to find
will help new thoughts arise,
where all the single lights that burn
combine their angled rays
till by their gathered light we learn
to give you thanks and praise.

WE HAVE MET CHRIST

56 | We Have Met Christ
Raised and Living

We have met Christ raised and living
in the people we have known.
Through their acts of grace and giving
God's incarnate light has shone:
Christ our savior, Christ our friend,
life and love that never end!

When the Word of God was spoken
and baptismal waters poured
and the bread of life was broken,
we received whom we adored:
Christ our savior, Christ our friend,
life and love that never end!

When we wept with families weeping
and we stood where they must stand,
all our strength was drawn by keeping
hold of Christ's assuring hand:
Christ our savior, Christ our friend,
life and love that never end!

When the seeds of faith we planted
started taking deeper root
it was Christ whose presence granted
growth that bore the Spirit's fruit:
Christ our savior, Christ our friend,
life and love that never end!

And whenever we retreated
out of grief or hurt or fear
and we felt our faith defeated,
Christ reached out and held us near:
Christ our savior, Christ our friend,
life and love that never end!

Now this day when hearts are flowing
we give thanks in song and prayer
that in ways past human knowing
we're forever in Christ's care:
Christ our savior, Christ our friend,
life and love that never end!

57 | How Much We Owe to Those Who Live

How much we owe to those who live
the love of God each day,
whose faith and words and actions give
a witness to God's way:
the parents who awake at night
to soothe our infant tears,
the friends who judge not wrong or right
but share our doubts and fears.

They are the saints who walk with us
in shadows dark and deep,
who fill our mortal, anxious dust
with visions that can sweep
our souls beyond the narrow range
of what we daily see,
that grant to us the grace to change
and bring new worlds to be.

The saints who live on earth are one
with those who live above.
Together they help us become
a witness to the love
that angels and archangels sing,
that we ourselves have known
when we become an offering
to you, our God, alone.

58 | Look Who Gathers at Christ's Table!

Look who gathers at Christ's table!
Hear the stories that they bring.
Some are weeping, some are laughing
some have songs they want to sing.
Others ask why they're invited,
burdened by the wrong they've done.
Christ insists they all are welcome.
There is room for everyone.

Clouds of light surround the table,
ancient followers appear,
saints confessing how they wrestled
with their guilt, their doubt and fear.
Peter tells of his denying
Christ was ever in his sight,
Paul relates his fruitless efforts
to obliterate the light.

Their sad stories are repeated
in a thousand different ways,
but they share one thing in common:
they all end in thanks and praise
for the host who has invited
north and south and east and west
to converge around this table
where all life is fed and blest.

Bring your joy and bring your sadness,
and prepare to be surprised
by the host whose hands are wounded,
who will open wide your eyes
when he blesses bread and breaks it—
truth and manna from above!—
and then passes wine that wakens
in your heart the taste of love.

59 | We Look Down Deep to Look Out Far

We look down deep to look out far
for in the heart's deep caves
we find the Light that lights each star,
its particles and waves.
O Light that shines in everyone
but burns yet brighter still
in Christ and all that Christ has done,
help us to do your will.

We look out far to look down deep
for in the swirling skies
we sense the wind whose breathings sweep
the heart as wordless sighs.
O Wind that blows in all that lives
but sends its strongest gust
through Christ and through the life Christ gives,
fill us with hope and trust.

We look where all directions merge,
where heart and heaven meet,
where light and wind as one converge
to make our prayer complete:
O burn and blow in every place
down deep and far above
till Christ and Christ's transforming grace
transfigure all through love.

Notes on Meter, Scriptural References, and Occasion

Numbers refer to the title number, not the page number.

1. Above the Moon Earth Rises
   meter: 7-6-7-6 D
   scripture: Genesis 1, Psalms 8, 19, 24, 104
   occasion: Services on ecology, thanksgiving, stewardship

2. God Saw that Earth Was Good
   meter: 6-6-8-6 D (SMD)
   scripture: Genesis 1 and 2
   occasion: Services on creation and humanity

3. Aspen at Dusk
   meter: Irregular
   scripture: Isaiah 40:6
   occasion: Meditating on the glitter of Aspen
            in light of Isaiah's realism

4. How Bright the Dawn, the Sun's First Ray
   meter: 8-6-8-6 (CM)
   scripture: Psalm 30:5
   occasion: A children's hymn

5. Each Breath is Borrowed Air
   meter: 6-6-8-6 D (SMD)
   scripture: Genesis 2:7, Psalm 150:6, Isaiah 42:5
   occasion: Thanksgiving, praise, wonder at life

6. Wind over the Plain
   meter: Irregular
   scripture: Genesis 2:7, Acts 2
   occasion: Pentecost, an invocation

7. What Wind Would Carry?
   meter: Irregular
   scripture: None
   occasion: Sending flowers to one far away

8. I Love a Hint of Winter
   meter: Irregular
   scripture: Psalm 90:10
   occasion: Meditating on our mortality

9. Angels Visit when We Sing
   meter: 7-7-7-7 with Alleluias
   scripture: Job 38:7, Luke 2:8–14, Luke 24:1–7
   occasion: Christmas, Easter, celebrating
              ministries of music

10. Sing to God as Sings the Ocean
    meter: 8-7-8-7 D
    scripture: Psalm 30:5, John 4:14, Romans 8:26–27
    occasion: Celebrating ministries of music

11. The Crickets Chanting through the Night
    meter: 8-7-8-7 D
    scripture: Psalm 104
    occasion: Celebrating religious arts

12. By Mortal Love Our Hearts Are Drawn
    meter: 8-6-8-6 D (CMD)
    scripture: John 4:14, 1 John 4:7–11
    occasion: Sermons on love, weddings

13. Love is a Thin Flame
    meter: Irregular
    scripture: None. An aria from a libretto for a grand opera, "An
               Island of Sand." The opera takes place in a neo-gothic
               church that is under reconstruction. The church sexton
               is the central character, Tashika Tumsigali, a woman
               from a tropical island who at the opera's conclusion
               laments the ways she has been betrayed by those who
               loved her.
    occasion: Sermons on broken relationships

14. Love Simple Things to Train the Heart
    meter: 8-6-8-6 D (CMD)
    scripture: None in particular; focus is the Trinity
               as a pattern of love
    occasion: Trinity Sunday

15. Seeded in the Stars
    meter: Irregular
    scripture: Genesis 1
    occasion: Celebrating justice for all sexual orientations

16. Jesu, Jesu
    meter: Regular but highly varied line lengths
               and accented patterns
    scripture: Mark 11:1–11
    occasion: Palm Sunday. This is a folk anthem from
               the libretto for an opera, "An Island of Sand" (see #13
               in this index).

17. With Holy Anger, Christ
    meter: Irregular
    scripture: Mark 11:15–19, John 2:13–17
    occasion: Holy Week, sermons on healthy anger and justice

18. Yes, I Know We Both Agreed
    meter: Irregular
    scripture: John 2:1–11
    occasion: Sermons on sacraments in common life, marriage

19. Let Jove Rise from His Couch of Clouds
    meter: Irregular
    scripture: John 1:1–18
    occasion: Sermons about incarnation versus untouched deity

20. Born in a Barn where Cows and Sheep
    meter: 8-7-7-7
    scripture: Matthew 2:16–18, Luke 2:1–7
    occasion: Christmas

21. Disturbed by Light
    meter: 8-8-8-8 with refrain of 8-8 (LM)
    scripture: Luke 2:8–14, Matthew 2:1–12
    occasion: Christmas, Incarnation

22. Angel and Star
    meter: 4-4-4-4
    scripture: Luke 2:8–14, Matthew 2:1–12
    occasion: Christmas

23. Cameo Angel
    meter: Irregular
    scripture: Luke 1:26–38, Luke 2:1–14
    occasion: Christmas

24. Are You a Shepherd?
    meter: 5-4-5-4 with refrain 4-6-5-5
    scripture: Matthew 2, Luke 2:1–20
    occasion: Christmas

25. One Gift the Magi Bore
    meter: 6-6-8-6 (SM)
    scripture: Matthew 2:1–12
    occasion: Epiphany

26. Directions for Magi
    meter: 6-6-8-6 (SM)
    scripture: Matthew 2:1–12
    occasion: Epiphany

27. God Weeps with Us Who Weep and Mourn
    meter: 8-6-8-6 D (CMD)
    scripture: Romans 12:15
    occasion: Funerals, especially for those who
              have died from AIDS

28. Cradle Lament
    meter: Irregular
    scripture: Isaiah 40:6
    occasion: Sermons on the transitory character of life

29. Come in Silence, Named but Nameless
    meter: Irregular
    scripture: Exodus 20:7
    occasion: Sermons on the misuse of God's
              name to oppress others

30. Traveler, Are You Passing Through?
    meter: 7-7-7-7 D
    scripture: Luke 24:13–35
    occasion: Easter, communion, welcoming newcomers

31. We're Sailing, We're Sailing
    meter: Irregular
    scripture: None. A love duet from the libretto for an opera,
              "An Island of Sand" (see #13 in this index).
    occasion: Weddings, funerals

32. Come with Moses to the Mountain
    meter: 8-7-8-7 D
    scripture: Exodus 3:1–15, Mark 9:2–8 and parallels
    occasion: Transfiguration Sunday, sermons on faith as journey

33. Come to the Mountain
    meter: Irregular
    scripture: Exodus 3:1–15, Isaiah 2:4, Isaiah 11:1–9,
              Isaiah 60, Mark 9:2-8
    occasion: Transfiguration Sunday, sermons on faith as
              journey. All sections can be done at once or
              scattered through the liturgy

34. Come, Join Us as We Journey
    meter: 7-6-7-6 D
    scripture: Genesis 12:1–4, Luke 24:13–35
    occasion: Sermons on faith as a journey, church anniversaries

35. The Land Promises More to the Eye
    meter: Irregular
    scripture: Philippians 1:21–24
    occasion: Sermons that recognize how the yearnings
              of the heart transfigure the earth

36. From Many Different Ancient Springs
    meter: 8-6-8-6 D (CMD with refrain)
    scripture: Passages from any religious tradition using water
    occasion: Ecumenical and inter-religious gatherings

37. Somewhere I Have Never Traveled
    meter: Irregular
    scripture: None. Instead, St. Augustine: "Our hearts are
              restless until they find their rest in Thee, O Lord."
    occasion: Sermons on the yearning of the human heart

38. Welcome, Welcome! The Door is Open
    meter: 9-6-8-6 with refrain
    scripture: Luke 13:29
    occasion: Sermons on Eucharist, communion, hospitality

39. Through Our Beating Hearts Remind Us
    meter: 8-7-8-7 D
    scripture: Genesis 1 and 2
    occasion: Sermons on thanksgiving and stewardship

40. Thanks Be to God for Teachers
    meter: 3-8-8-8 with refrain
    scripture: Psalm 78
    occasion: Recognition of teachers

41. Obelisks, Stelae, Sculpted Sarcophagi
    meter: Irregular
    scripture: Philippians 4:8
    occasion: Sermons on friendship, enduring values

42. Two Poems from Those Who Have Lost Language
    meter: Irregular
    scripture: None
    occasion: Sermons on communication and stroke

43. It is Lonely
    meter: Irregular
    scripture: Luke 16:26. An aria from the libretto for an opera,
               "An Island of Sand" (see #13 in this index).
    occasion: Funerals

44. Safe Landing on a Distant Shore
    meter: 8-6-8-6 (CM)
    scripture: Matthew 14:22–33
    occasion: Funerals

45. For God Risk Everything!
    meter: 6-6-8-6 D (SMD)
    scripture Matthew 25:14–30
    occasion: Sermons on discipleship

46. To My Equestrian Friend
    meter: Irregular
    scripture: Proverbs 22:6
    occasion: Encouraging a teenager's great dreams

47. We Live in that Far Future
     meter: 7-6-7-6 D
     scripture: 1 Corinthians 15:51–54 and many passages
                on the church
     occasion: Anniversary of a church

48. The Bush in Flame but not Consumed
     meter: 8-6-8-6 D (CMD)
     scripture: Exodus 3:1–15
     occasion: Ordinations. There is a hymn with the same
                first line in *Borrowed Light,* but otherwise this
                is an entirely new hymn.

49. God, Whose Word from Age to Age
     meter: 7-8-7-8 with refrain
     scripture: Hebrews 13:8
     occasion: Church or denominational anniversary

50. The Church under Reconstruction
     meter: Irregular
     scripture: Post-exilic passages dealing with the Temple's
                destruction, for example: Psalm 137
     occasion: Sermons seeking to construct new understandings
                of God, faith, and church

51. Christ Still Walks These Wooded Hills
     meter: 7-7-7-7 D
     scripture: Synoptic gospel portraits of Christ
     occasion: Church anniversary, Pentecost

52. As the Seed that Cleaves a Stone
     meter: 7-7-7-7 D
     scripture: Matthew 17:20
     occasion: Sermons celebrating the place of art, science,
                and thought in the life of faith

53. Where the Cross Still Casts its Shadow
     meter: 8-7-8-7 D
     scripture: 1 Corinthians 1:18
     occasion: Church anniversary

54. Put Out from Shore to Cast Your Nets
     meter: 8-6-8-6 (CM with refrain)
     scripture: Luke 5:1–11
     occasion: Church anniversary, new mission, discipleship

55. Like Stars Positioned Far Apart
    meter: 8-6-8-6 D (CMD)
    scripture: Any text about creation or knowledge
    occasion: Sermons on the relationship of science, faith, and art

56. We Have Met Christ Raised and Living
    meter: 8-7-8-7-7-7
    scripture: Luke 24:13–35
    occasion: Celebration of a ministry

57. How Much We Owe to Those Who Live
    meter: 8-6-8-6 D (CMD)
    scripture: 1 Corinthians 14:33 and Hebrews 12:1–2
    occasion: All Saints Day

58. Look Who Gathers at Christ's Table!
    meter: 8-7-8-7 D
    scripture: Luke 13:29
    occasion: Communion/Eucharist, ecumenical celebrations

59. We Look Down Deep to Look Out Far
    meter: 8-6-8-6 D (CMD)
    scripture: Psalm 19 and Romans 8: 26–27
    occasion: Opening of a school year, sermons on
                science and spirituality

Metrical Index

Index by Scriptural Reference

Index by Theme and Image

Index by First Line and Title

Most, but not all titles are the first line. Initial line of text is in italics.